MONEY AT YOUR COMMAND!

Money at Your Command!

SHIRLEY SMOLKO, MBA, MSA

Cavallaro Publishing

CONTENTS

First Printing, 2022

Second Printing, 2023

ISBN: 978-1-958104-02-6

Library of Congress Control Number: 2022907895

Cavallaro Publishing
North Venice, Florida
www.cavallaropub.com
cavallaropub@gmail.com

DISCLAIMER

This book contains material from a distant time that may not be gender-neutral or sensitive. Therefore, all pronouns shall be deemed to refer to the masculine, feminine, neuter, singular, or plural; wherever used herein, a pronoun in the masculine gender shall be considered to include the feminine gender.

The publisher and the author do not make any guarantees or other promises as to any results that may be obtained from using the contents of this book. To the maximum extent permitted by law, the publisher and the author disclaim any and all liability in the event any information, commentary, analysis, opinions, advice, or recommendations contained in this book prove to be inaccurate, incomplete, or unreliable or result in any losses.

In summary, you understand that we make absolutely no guarantees as a result of applying this information, as well as the fact that you are solely responsible for the results of any action taken on your part as a result of any given information.

YOUR WORD IS YOUR WAND!

Your word is your wand, filled with magic and power! You have the power to change an unhappy situation by waving the wand of your words over it. Instead of sorrow, you can have joy; instead of sickness, you can have health; instead of lack, you can have plenty.

In her book, *Your Word is Your Wand*, *Florence Scovel Shinn* writes about a woman who came to her for a prosperity treatment. This lady possessed just two dollars in the whole world (not a bad amount to have in your wallet in 1928, but that was the total of everything she had). Florence spoke the following command over the lady's purse:

> *We bless the two dollars and know that you have the magic purse of the Spirit; it can never be depleted. As money goes out, immediately money comes in, under grace in perfect ways. I see it always crammed, jammed with money: yellow bills, green bills, pink checks, blue*

1

checks, white checks, gold, silver, and currency. I see it bulging with abundance!

Shortly afterward, the lady was given a gift of six thousand dollars. Fearless faith and the spoken word brought it to pass. The affirmation of the magic purse is very powerful because it conveys a clear picture to the subconscious mind of what is being commanded. Also, it is impossible not to see your purse or wallet filled with money when using the words *crammed* and *jammed.*

Visualization is the creative faculty; therefore, it is important to choose words that bring a flash of fulfillment to the command. Never force a picture, but let the divine idea or picture of it flash into your conscious mind.

There is no truth in lack or limitation. Your word is your wand, and you have the power to transmute poverty into wealth. Your universal supply is endless, and all your commands manifest with ease! Money is at your command!

~ 2 ~

THE CREATIVE WORD

The whole universe is alive with cosmic intelligence; it is Infinite Creative Mind at work. The mind gives birth to thought and then uses thought as the model for its creation. The mind, whether universal or individual, has only one way to initiate the act of creation, and that is through thought, which in turn always expresses itself in words. We always think in concrete terms or words. In the Bible, we are told in John 1:1-3:

> *In the beginning was the Word, and the Word was with God, and the Word was God. ² He was with God in the beginning. ³ Through him, all things were made; without him, nothing was made that has been made. (NIV)*

It is written in Psalms 33:7-9:

> *By the word of the LORD were the heavens made, and their starry hosts by the breath of his mouth. He gathers*

the waters of the sea into jars; he puts the deep into store-
houses. Let all the earth fear the LORD; let all the people
of the world revere him. For he spoke, and it came to be;
he commanded, and it stood firm. (NIV)

The study of quantum physics suggests that the nature of primal substance (or ether) is that all its particles are in perfect equilibrium or balance. The only way this balance can be disturbed and brought into form is by the application of some immaterial force to primal substance. In his paper, *Man's Greatest Achievement*, Nikola Tesla wrote:

The primary substance, thrown into infinitesimal whirls
of prodigious velocity, becomes gross matter; the force
subsides, the motion ceases, and matter disappears, re-
verting to the primary substance.

We must therefore posit that there is a power brought about by will, or the act of Mind, as the only immaterial force responsible for bringing about manifestation in the physical world. In his book *Thought Power, Sri* Swami Sivananda wrote:

Thought is the greatest force on earth. Thought is the most
powerful weapon in the armor of a yogi. Constructive
thought transforms, renews, and builds. The far-reaching
possibilities of this force were most accurately developed
to perfection by the ancients and put to the highest pos-
sible use. For thought is the primal force at the origin and
back of all creation; the genesis of the entire phenomenal

creation is given as a single thought that arose in the Cosmic Mind. The world is the Primal Idea made manifest. This First Thought became manifest as a vibration issuing from the Eternal Stillness of the Divine Essence. This is the reference in classic terminology to the Ichha, the desire of the Hiranyagarbha, the Cosmic Soul, that originates as a Spandana, or vibration. This vibration is nothing like the rapid oscillation to and fro of physical particles, but is something infinitely subtle, so subtle as to be even inconceivable to the normal mind. But this has made it clear that all forces are ultimately resolvable into a state of pure vibration. Modern science has also recently arrived at this conclusion after its prolonged research on external physical nature.

Later in the book, he goes on to say:

Thought is a vital, living, dynamic power—the most vital, subtle, and irresistible force existing in the universe. Through the instrumentality of thought, you acquire creative power. Thought passes from one man to another. It influences people; a man of powerful thought can easily influence people of weak thought.

Life can only come from life, and motion can only have its origin in the mind. The word spirit comes from the Latin root 'spiro, which is also the Italian word for 'I breathe. Therefore, the universe springs from the outbreathing of the Mind. This is the expansive movement of spirit with which ancient philosophers deal so much. We are told in

Genesis 1:2: — "The spirit of God moved on the face of the waters." The word "waters" is the esoteric term for Mind or Creative Mind. The Word acts on the Universal Mind to produce substance in the visible universe and then to bring that substance into varied forms, in the sun, moon, stars, land, sea, vegetation, and man.

So we find that the Mind acts by thought; thought expresses itself in words, and we may go one step further and say that words are expressed by the voice. Therefore, all ancient writers dealt much with the voice: "The voice of the Lord is upon many waters." The Sanskrit writings speak of Vach; the Latin is Vox, or voice. In other words, the objective universe, which is made up of motion or vibration in some form or another, begins with the voice. Until the voice speaks, the universe exists only in the Creative Mind. As soon as Creative Mind selects a place to begin the creation of a universe, it then starts motion or vibration by the voice. The whole objective world can be explained as a vibration in some form or another. Everything from the gold in your computer to the light in the sun, from the chair you sit on to the brain in your head, is composed of particles of substance pulsating at different rates of vibration. All material things can be divided into atoms and theoretically dissolved into ether. Ether is simply another name for Mind. The electron is energy. The ultimate substance of which all things are made is the same. Physical differences in this substance occur due to the arrangement of atomic particles as well as their rate of motion. William Hayes Ward once stated, "The whole great universe of starry worlds is one, built out of the same materials, moved by the same forces, and governed by the same physical law." This one substance is Mind, and the one force is thought, which becomes concrete in words and expresses itself in voice or vibration. A voice is only an intelligible vibration or purposeful sound. Again, the purposeful sound must be the word. We can easily conclude that the creative principle is the word.

~ 3 ~

YOUR CREATIVE WORD

We share the nature of God. Our thoughts act on Original Substance. Every word we speak, whether shallow or deep, is a creative word. That is why we are told in Matthew 12:37 of the Bible, "By your words you will be justified, and by your words you will be condemned."

You control your destiny through the thoughts you have. Therefore, it is imperative for you to achieve wealth consciousness if you want to manifest abundance and prosperity. Let go of any tendency to speak critically of rich people, and do not damn yourself, your friends, or your work with words of pessimism. Through the Law of Command, the words you speak are alive and creative. Believe you have a right to be rich, and make it so!

Faith: The Substance of Things Commanded

Now faith is the substance of things hoped for; it is the evidence of things not seen (Hebrews 11:1 NIV). Faith is an attitude of confident expectancy. It is not a creed or religion; it is steady confidence. Faith connects the immediate present with the immediate future. It is certain knowledge that has not yet reached the point of demonstration where it can be subjected to the ordinary tests of logic and experience but is just as certain of itself as though it could. It is the positive conviction not only that the real is derived from the good and the good from the real, but also that the best will happen to me and mine both now and in the days to come.

Faith is unwavering belief. It requires that you ignore all appearances contrary to your creative word while concentrating on that which you desire. It will always be argued that *facts* speak for themselves and can't be refuted. This is nonsense; in reality, facts are transient rather than stable. Whatever you do, always remember that your cosmic source of power is prepared to help you alter the facts at your command. All you have to do is provide a channel of belief (faith) through which this may work. For example, you might say to me, *I have no money because it is my lot in life.* What is actually at work here is a deep-rooted belief that is producing poverty. There is a choice: you could stay poverty-stricken by continuing to believe in the 'apparent facts, or you could ignore the *apparent facts* and command Original Substance to bring you wealth. What you must do is change your beliefs and connect to abundant power by opening up a channel. Once you have decided to do so, you hold fast to the new belief while ignoring the 'apparent facts. Never let the 'apparent facts' dictate how you run your life, and never allow them to become the basis for belief.

Faith is the star that glimmers in what would otherwise be darkness. It is a higher perceptive power of the mind—a finer sense—that allows us to perceive things that are possible. The faith of yesterday is experienced today and made history tomorrow. By faith, inventions are created, people land on the moon, and vast fortunes are made.

~ 4 ~

COMMANDING MONEY
WITH YOUR SPOKEN WORD

The word *command* means to have authority or control. Through the Law of Command, you can create all the money you need to experience the good life. Never underestimate the power of your words. With your words, you have created your present reality. If you have created a life of lack and limitation with your previous words, you can change your financial circumstances—starting today —by commanding money and prosperity to come to you.

This is the long-awaited section of the book where I actually share with you a powerful technique for using words to command the manifestation of money and prosperity. This technique is based on an ancient metaphysical method known as incantation. The use of Incantation involves the speaking or singing of words that are believed to have the power to manifest desired results. The use of incantation to effect change is universally known since remote antiquity. Throughout the rest of the book,

I will be using the words *incantation* and *command* interchangeably.

Most cultures have some idea about words having supernatural constructive powers, but nowhere is this belief stronger than in Judaism. The incantation was the most prominent element in Jewish magick. Sometimes it was accompanied by ritual, but most of the time it was used alone because it was considered all-sufficient in itself to produce the desired effect. Both Christian and Jewish Kabbalists emphasize that God created the universe by means of a series of speech acts, and because we are made in the image of the Creator, we have the same power of speech to create or destroy.

The use of incantations is found in other cultures as well. There is evidence that in the early historical periods of both Greece and Rome, people believed in the efficacy of incantations. During the Hellenistic period, the magical use of incantation was very popular. In most magical papyri, incantations read almost like prayers but were believed to have inherent magical powers to accomplish results without the intervention of the gods or God.

Three standard types of incantations have been identified among the formulas used in different cultures. The primary type is the command form, which uses imperatives or statements of obligation to bind spiritual powers to the desired action. The second type uses declarations in the form of affirmations to establish the hoped-for result. The third type uses the prayer mode of beseeching God or another spiritual power to take the desired action.

The first type of incantation uses an imperative

statement or phrase to give a direct command. Imperative phrases do not have a subject; instead, a directive is given to an implied second person. For example, the sentence "Wash your laundry" commands the implied subject to wash their clothes.

The second type of incantation uses a declarative statement to perform the intended result. A declarative statement is a sentence that states a fact pertaining to the present or future. Affirmations are declarations that state something as being true.

The third type of incantation is that of beseeching or charming the sacred powers to act benevolently. Beseech means to beg urgently or anxiously. It usually takes the form of a petitioning prayer. The following prayer is a good example: "God, if it be your will, please give me money for the rent." This type of incantation is usually not effective because it lacks an important ingredient in magick and manifestation—faith. Needless to say, we will not be using this type of incantation. We will be using imperative and declarative statements; both have been found to be very effective in producing results. You can use incantations written by someone else or write your own. Just make sure that the incantation used resonates with you and that you really believe in what you're saying.

~ 5 ~

CHARGING YOUR WORDS
WITH POWER

Not every word we speak has the power to create. For instance, saying hi to your neighbor is a salutation, not a command. Most of the words we speak in our daily lives are conversational and not intended to magically bring about a desired result. To make your command super effective, you will need to charge your words with power and intention. I have found that visualization is the best way to accomplish this. The following exercise will help you relax so you can contact and communicate with the power center of your subconscious mind.

Charging Exercise

Step #1: Relaxing the Body and Mind Through Diaphragmatic Breathing

The first step in creative visualization is to relax your body and mind. Relaxing your body and mind allows you to achieve the alpha brainwave level, which produces the perfect state for impressing your subconscious mind. It's my opinion that diaphragmatic breathing is the perfect technique for achieving relaxation to prepare you for your creative visualization session. You can perform this creative visualization either sitting up or lying down.

To perform this exercise while sitting in a chair:

- Sit comfortably with your feet on the floor, and avoid slouching. Make sure your shoulders, head, and neck are relaxed.

- Place one hand on your upper chest and the other just below your rib cage. This will allow you to feel your diaphragm move as you breathe.

- Breathe in slowly through your nose so that your stomach moves out against your hand. The hand on your chest should remain as still as possible.

- Tighten your stomach muscles, letting them fall inward as you exhale through pursed lips. The hand on your upper chest must remain as still as possible.

To perform this exercise while lying down:

- Lie on your back on a flat surface (or in bed)

with your knees bent. You can use a pillow under your head and your knees for support if that's more comfortable.

• Place one hand on your upper chest and the other on your belly, just below your rib cage.

• Breathe in slowly through your nose, letting the air in deeply, towards your lower belly. The hand on your chest should remain still, while the one on your belly should rise.

• Tighten your abdominal muscles and let them fall inward as you exhale through pursed lips. The hand on your belly should move back to its original position.

Step #2: Power Visualization

When you feel deeply relaxed, imagine a ball of white light in the center of your abdomen and watch as it travels up your body and into your mouth. This ball of light permeates your tongue, which now glows with intense white light. Your tongue says to you, "The words I speak have the power to accomplish that which I command." At the end of your visualization, slowly open your eyes and wiggle your fingers and toes. Now you are ready to make your command!

~ 6 ~

IMPERATIVE COMMANDS

Remember to do the charging exercise before stating your imperative commands. When using commands, it is not necessary to repeat them a certain number of times or use a certain tone of voice. Always do what resonates with you. Do not make your incantations more difficult than they need to be. Keep your incantations as specific and simple as possible. If you need a specific amount of money within a certain amount of time, make sure you specify it within the incantation. It is also a good idea to include in your statement that the money must come in ways that harm no one.

Listed below are some money commands you can use to get started. Feel free to amend them to suit your needs, or you can write your own from scratch:

- Money, Money come to me with harm to none, so let it be!

- Money, Money come to me three times more than I need!

- I summon money from everywhere, so I can live without a care.

- Money luck I draw you in. May I never worry again!

- Waves of cash come to me. With harm to none, as I will so mote it be.

- Sky above and earth below, See my money grow and grow.

- All the money I need, come quickly to me. With harm to none, so let it be!

- I call upon the money stream. With harm to none, as I will so let it be!

- $300,000 in sales I receive, as I will so mote it be!

- $8,000 for my truck I receive, as I will so let it be!

- $3,000 in cash through grace and ease with harm to none within a week I receive!

- $900,000 in cash for my house within a week I'll receive, and my buyer will be very pleased!

Although most of the incantations I have listed above rhyme, they do not have to rhyme in order to work. Rhyming sounds nice to the ear because it has a *sing-song* attribute to it, but it is definitely not necessary for achieving results. The most important element is to believe that you have what you say. Our job is not to understand how these things are brought to us, but to believe that the end result of what we command will be manifested for us.

~ 7 ~

DECLARATIVE COMMANDS

To affirm means "to make firm. An affirmation is a strong, positive statement that something is already so. Using affirmations is one of the easiest ways to invoke the Law of Command. You can use those listed below or write your own.

- I experience positive cash flow as a key part of my life.

- I will overcome any financial obstacles that stand in my way.

- I accomplish all of my financial goals.

- I am living my financial dream.

- Money is good and very good. I have lots of money, and that's a blessing.

- It is easy and natural for me to command money.

- I am prosperous and successful.

- My life is filled with wealth and money.

- An abundance of money flows to me with ease. I deserve and accept it.

- I accept and receive pleasant, unexpected cash flows.

- I accept and receive unexpected channels of prosperity.

- I always have more than enough money to do with as I please.

- I deserve to have more money, and it is so.

- I am always discovering new streams of income.

- Money comes my way in both expected and unexpected ways.

- I am open to receiving all the wealth life brings to me.

- The appearance of poverty in my life is unreal. I can change my financial situation at any time I choose.

- Money ideas flow freely to me, and I am able to open new channels of money at any time.

- I'm getting out of my own way when it comes to money by allowing divine money ideas to come to me.

- The money I need always comes to me in a timely manner when I need it.

- I know how to invoke the energy of money, and money comes to me easily at my command.

- I have the magic purse of the Spirit; it can never be depleted. As money goes out, immediately money comes in, under grace in perfect ways.

Affirmations have helped many people make significant changes in their lives. But they don't always work for everyone. How is it that one person can have great success using this tool while others may not experience any results at all? Affirmations only work when an individual is able to consciously suspend disbelief in order to program the subconscious mind. The subconscious doesn't know the difference between what is real and what is imaginary.

When you watch a movie and you start to laugh or cry, your mind believes the plot even though it is fiction. This is known as suspension of disbelief, and this is what you must do for affirmations to work. You have to believe the statements are true, whether they appear to be true or not. Think of it as writing a new movie script for your life.

~ 8 ~

INCANTATIONS USING THE PSALMS

For thousands of years, the Book of Psalms has been used with surprising results to help solve many of the problems that arise in life. Jewish Mystics, Christian Mystics, Cabalists; Hoodoo Practitioners, and Pow Wow Practitioners (those who practice Pennsylvania Dutch Folk Magick) have used the Psalms extensively with great success. I have personally found that just meditating on the Book of Psalms is very effective in obtaining desired results, and speaking them aloud is even more effective. I like to use as few phrases or sentences as possible when stating commands from the Psalms.

Reciting the book of Psalms is a very powerful way to quickly change your financial situation. You do not have to be religious to use this sacred text. Just have faith in the words of these scriptures to release power. The Psalms create such a strong energy when read aloud that they can shift your vibration almost immediately. Over time, if you consistently use the Psalms in your spiritual practice, you will see drastic changes in your life.

Below, I have listed the financial Psalms that I have used and experienced amazing results with. Use all of the verses, but especially those that resonate with you or that you are drawn to. You can use the Book of Psalms for every aspect of your life, not just finances. There is a Psalm that can help you overcome every challenge you may face.

Psalms for Money to Flow Through Business Channels

Psalm 1:3

3. That person is like a tree planted by streams of water, which yields its fruit in season and whose leaf does not wither—whatever they do prospers.

Psalm 8:1-9

1. O Lord, our Lord, your majestic name fills the earth!

Your glory is higher than the heavens.

2. You have taught children and infants to tell of your strength.

silencing your enemies and all who oppose you.

3. When I look at the night sky and see the work of your fingers, the moon and the stars you set in place.

4. What are mere mortals that you should think about?

human beings that you should care for them?

5. Yet you made them only a little lower than God and crowned them with glory and honor.

6. You gave them charge of everything you made, putting all things under their authority.

7. the flocks, the herds, and all the wild animals,

8. The birds in the sky, the fish in the sea, and everything that swims in the ocean currents

9. O Lord, our Lord, your majestic name fills the earth!

Psalm 37:4-5

4. Delight yourself also in the Lord, and He shall give you the desires of your heart.

5. Commit your way to the Lord; trust also in Him, and He shall bring it to pass.

Psalm 65:9-13

9. You care for the land and water it; you enrich it abundantly.

The streams of God are filled with water to provide the people with grain, for so you have ordained it.

10. You drench its furrows and level its ridges; you soften it with showers and bless its crops.

11. You crown the year with your bounty, and your carts overflow with abundance.

12. The grasslands of the wilderness overflow; the hills are clothed with gladness.

13. The meadows are covered with flocks, and the valleys are mantled with grain; they shout for joy and sing.

Psalm 85:12-13

12. The Lord will indeed give what is good, and our land will yield its harvest.

13. Righteousness goes before him and prepares the way for his steps.

Psalm 115:14-16

14. May the Lord cause you to flourish, both you and your children.

15. May you be blessed by the Lord, the Maker of heaven and earth.

16. *The highest heavens belong to the Lord, but the earth he has given to mankind.*

Psalms for Attracting Money and Good Fortune

Psalm 4:6-7

6. *Many, Lord, are asking, "Who will bring us prosperity? Let the light of your face shine on us.*

7. *Fill my heart with joy when their grain and new wine abound.*

Psalm 28:8-9

8. *The Lord is the strength of his people, a fortress of salvation for his anointed one.*

9. *Save your people and bless your inheritance; be their shepherd and carry them forever.*

Psalm 34:10

10. *The lions may grow weak and hungry, but those who seek the Lord will lack no good thing.*

Psalm 35:27

27. Let them shout for joy and be glad, who favor my righteous cause; and let them say continually,

"Let the Lord be magnified, who has pleasure in the prosperity of His servant.

Psalm 57:9-10

9. I will praise you, Lord, among the nations; I will sing of you among the peoples.

10. For great is your love, reaching to the heavens; your faithfulness reaches to the skies.

Psalm 67:1&6

1. The land yields its harvest, and God, our God, blesses us.

6. The land yields its harvest; God, our God, blesses us.

Psalms 112:3

3. Wealth and riches are in their houses, and their righteousness endures forever.

Psalm 113:7 & 8

7. He raises the poor from the dust and lifts the needy from the ash heap:

8. He seats them with princes, with the princes of his people.

Psalm 115:14

114. May the Lord cause you to flourish, both you and your children.

Psalm 118:25

25. Lord, save us! Lord, grant us success!

Psalm 122:7

7. Peace be within your walls, prosperity within your palaces.

Psalms for Getting Money Fast

Psalm 35:10

10. My whole being will exclaim, "Who is like you, Lord? You rescue the poor from those too strong for them, the poor and needy from those who rob them."

Psalm 68:19

19. Blessed be the Lord, who daily loads us with benefits.

Psalm 69:32-33

32. The poor will see and be glad—you who seek God, may your hearts live!

33. The Lord hears the needy and does not despise his captive people.

Psalm 72:15-16

15. Long may he live! May the gold from Sheba be given to him. May people ever pray for him and bless him all day long.

16. May grain abound throughout the land; on the tops of the hills, may it sway. May the crops flourish like Lebanon and thrive like the grass in the field.

Psalm 82:3&4

3. Defend the weak and the fatherless; uphold the cause of the poor and the oppressed.

4. Rescue the weak and the needy; deliver them from the hand of the wicked.

Psalms to Stop the Loss of Money

Psalm 23:1

1. The Lord is my shepherd; I shall not want.

Psalm 72:3-7

3. May the mountains bring prosperity to the people, The hills are the fruit of righteousness.

4. May he defend the afflicted among the people?

and save the children of the needy;
May he crush the oppressor.

5. May he endure as long as the sun,
as long as the moon, through all generations.

6. May he be like rain falling on a mown field,
like showers watering the earth.

7. In his days, may the righteous flourish.
and prosperity abound till the moon is no more.

Psalm 92:12-14

12. The righteous will flourish like a palm tree; they will grow like a cedar of Lebanon.

13. Planted in the house of the Lord, they will flourish in the courts of our God.

14. They will still bear fruit in old age; they will stay fresh and green.

There is no set formula for how to recite the Psalms. In other words, it really does not matter what time of day you recite them, and there is no set number of repetitions that you must make. The most important element in the efficacy of reciting the Psalms is that you believe that there is power in them to manifest your desires. After reciting the Psalm out loud, visualize your command being manifested by the power of your words.

The Psalms are not the only scriptures you can use as incantations. There are scriptures throughout the Bible that are very effective in manifesting what you desire. We will take a look at these other scriptures in the next chapter.

~ 9 ~

BIBLE DECREES TO
ATTRACT MONEY

According to Merriam-Webster online, a decree is an order having the force of law. It also means to command or enjoin—to direct or impose by authoritative order or with urgent admonition. In her book *The Dynamic Laws of Prayer*, Catherine Ponder states the following about the power of words released through decrees:

> *The word is dynamic because it creates. Speech is the very breath of God because it creates. Nothing is more alive with power, and nothing has more creative power than affirmative words. This is true because words of truth have life, intelligence, and substance within them, which are released through decree.*

The following verses are very powerful in attracting money and prosperity. I have written decrees. In an attempt to personalize each verse, Quietly read and meditate on the

verse; then, state the associated decree out loud with conviction—believing that it is so!

Genesis 13:2

2. Abram was very rich in livestock, in silver, and in gold.

Decree: Abraham was rich, and so am I!

Genesis 13:5-6

5. Lot also, who went with Abram, had flocks, herds, and tents.

6. Now the land was not able to support them so that they might dwell together, for their possessions were so great that they could not dwell together.

Decree: And so it is with me!

Genesis 13:14-17

14. And the Lord said to Abram, after Lot had separated from him: "Lift your eyes now and look from the place where you are—northward, southward, eastward, and westward.

15. For all the land that you see, I give it to you and your descendants forever.

16. And I will make your descendants as the dust of the

earth, so that if a man could number the dust of the earth, then your descendants could also be numbered.

17. Arise, walk in the land through its length and its width, for I give it to you.

Decree: Land is given to me!

Genesis 39:23

23. The keeper of the prison did not look into anything that was under Joseph's authority because the Lord was with him, and whatever he did, the Lord made it prosper.

Decree: I am prospered in all I do!

Deuteronomy 2:7

7. For the Lord your God has blessed you in all the work of your hand. He knows you are trudging through this great wilderness. These forty years, the Lord your God has been with you; you have lacked nothing.

Decree: I am always cared for. I lack for nothing!

Deuteronomy 28:3-11

3. Blessed shall you be in the city, and blessed shall you be in the country. 4. Blessed shall be the fruit of your body, the produce of your ground, the increase of your herds, the increase of your cattle, and the offspring of your flocks.

5. Blessed shall be your basket and your kneading bowl.

6. Blessed shall you be when you come in, and blessed shall you be when you go out.

7. The Lord will cause your enemies who rise against you to be defeated before your face; they shall come out against you one way and flee before you seven ways.

8. The Lord will command the blessing on you in your storehouses and in all to which you set your hand, and He will bless you in the land which the Lord your God is giving you.

9. The Lord will establish you as a holy people to Himself, just as He has sworn to you, if you keep the commandments of the Lord your God and walk in His ways.

10. Then all the peoples of the earth shall see that you are called by the name of the Lord, and they shall be afraid of you.

11. And the Lord will grant you plenty of goods, in the fruit of your body, in the increase of your livestock, and in the produce of your ground, in the land that the Lord swore to your fathers to give you.

Decree: I am blessed with a great abundance of money and material goods!

Deuteronomy 30:19-20

19. I call heaven and earth witnesses today against you, that I have set before you life and death, blessing and cursing; therefore, choose life, that both you and your descendants may live.

20. That you may love the Lord your God, that you may obey His voice, and that you may cling to Him, for He is your life and the length of your days; and that you may dwell in the land which the Lord swore to your fathers, to Abraham, Isaac, and Jacob, to give them.

Decree: Today, I choose prosperity and a life full of blessings!

Joshua 1:8

8. This Book of the Law shall not depart from your mouth, but you shall meditate in it day and night, that you may observe to do according to all that is written in it. Then you will make your way prosperous, and then you will have good success.

Decree: My way is made prosperous, and I have good success!

1 Chronicles 29:12

12. Both riches and honor come from You, and You reign

*over all. In Your hand is power and might; in Your hand
is to make great and to give strength to all.*

Decree: I receive both riches and honor!

Proverbs 10:4

*4. He who has a slack hand becomes poor, but the hand of
the diligent is rich.*

Decree: My diligence makes me rich!

Ecclesiastes 5:19

*19. As for every man to whom God has given riches and
wealth and given him the power to eat of them, to receive his heritage, and to rejoice in his labor—this is the
gift of God.*

**Decree: The gift of wealth and riches is my
heritage!**

Philippians 4:19

*19. And my God shall supply all your needs according to
His riches in glory in Christ Jesus.*

Decree: I am amply supplied with all riches!

Hebrews 11:6

6. But without faith, it is impossible to please Him, for he

who comes to God must believe that He is and that He is a
rewarder of those who diligently seek Him.

Decree: I am rewarded with money and all man-
ner of prosperity!

James 1:17

17. Every good gift and every perfect gift is from above
and comes down from the Father of lights, with whom
there is no variation or shadow of turning.

Decree: I receive every good gift from above,
including money!

John 2

2. Beloved, I pray that you may prosper in all things and
be in health, just as your soul prospers.

Decree: My soul and finances prosper abun-
dantly!

You are a commander of money. Up to this point in your life, you may have been commanding the energy of money by default in accordance with beliefs that create lack and struggle. Starting today, you can use your authority and power to intentionally command money to manifest in substantial and increasing ways.

Contrary to the popular notion that seeing is believing, manifesting is all about believing in order to see. You really have to believe that you can have what you command, and believe it without a shadow of a doubt. Believe that your word is acted upon by an Almighty Power; feel the intensity of this great Power in and through all things you speak into it; and declare just what you wish it to do for you, never doubting in your mind but expecting that it will do just as you have directed it to.

About The Author

Shirley Smolko, also known as *The Venetian Medium*, is a natural Psychic Medium, which means she was born with the ability to perceive psychic information and communicate with the souls of people who have passed away. In addition to being a Psychic Medium, she is a publisher, author and lecturer.

She holds a Bachelor of Science in Nursing, a Masters in Business Administration, and another Masters degree in the Science of Accounting. She is also certified in grief counseling.

Shirley lives in the USA with her husband, Joe, and their two cats, Zoey and Cecilia. You can find out more about Shirley, her books, and what she is up to by going to: venetianmedium.com, or cavallaropub.com.

Books by Shirley Smolko (as of this printing):

- *My Adventures as a Psychic Nurse & Medium: Spirits Everywhere!* (Previously published as *Adventures of a Psychic Nurse: Spirits Everywhere!*)
- *My Adventures as a Psychic Nurse & Medium: Haunted Hospital!* (Previously published as: *More Adventures of a Psychic Nurse: Haunted Hospitals!*)
- *Just a Thought Away: Communicating With Loved Ones in Spirit*
- *Money Wants Me!*
- *Money at Your Command!*
- *Secret to the Science of Getting Rich*
- *At Your Command!*
- *Revelations of the Afterlife: A New Arrival*

- *Wisdom From the Wealthy Dead: A Medium Interviews the Souls of Three American Tycoons*

Be sure to look for more books to come!

www.ingramcontent.com/pod-product-compliance
Lightning Source LLC
Chambersburg PA
CBHW061325120626
46546CB00007B/2686